All About Penises

A Learning About Bodies Book

DORIAN SOLOT and **MARSHALL MILLER**

illustrated by **TYLER FEDER**

Henry Holt and Company

New York

To M, for asking good questions, and J,

for looking for answers

—D. S. & M. M.

For the kids who question and the grown-ups

who answer with honesty and care.

—T. F.

Henry Holt and Company, *Publishers since 1866*
Henry Holt® is a registered trademark of Macmillan Publishing Group, LLC
120 Broadway, New York, NY 10271 · mackids.com

Our books may be purchased in bulk for promotional, educational,
or business use. Please contact your local bookseller or the Macmillan
Corporate and Premium Sales Department at (800) 221-7945 ext. 5442
or by email at MacmillanSpecialMarkets@macmillan.com.

Library of Congress Control Number: 2023937724

First edition, 2024
Book design by Sharismar Rodriguez
Artwork rendered digitally with Procreate and Photoshop
Printed in China by R.R. Donnelley Asia Printing Solutions Ltd.,
Dongguan City, Guangdong Province

ISBN 978-1-250-85258-8
10 9 8 7 6 5 4 3 2 1

A NOTE FOR PARENTS AND CAREGIVERS

Why this book?

Many young children find penises confusing or surprising. Parents are sometimes unsure how to answer their questions in a way that's accurate, age-appropriate, and understandable. That's where *All About Penises* comes in.

This book recognizes that young children are seeking and deserve information beyond the mere existence of the body part. Kids notice that penises themselves are complex, and they note the silences and the absences: that genitals are generally not discussed, that most dolls have no genitals, and that penises are missing from books about belly buttons and songs about heads, shoulders, knees, and toes. This book is the one our friends and relatives told us they were searching for to read to their young children and to validate their questions and observations.

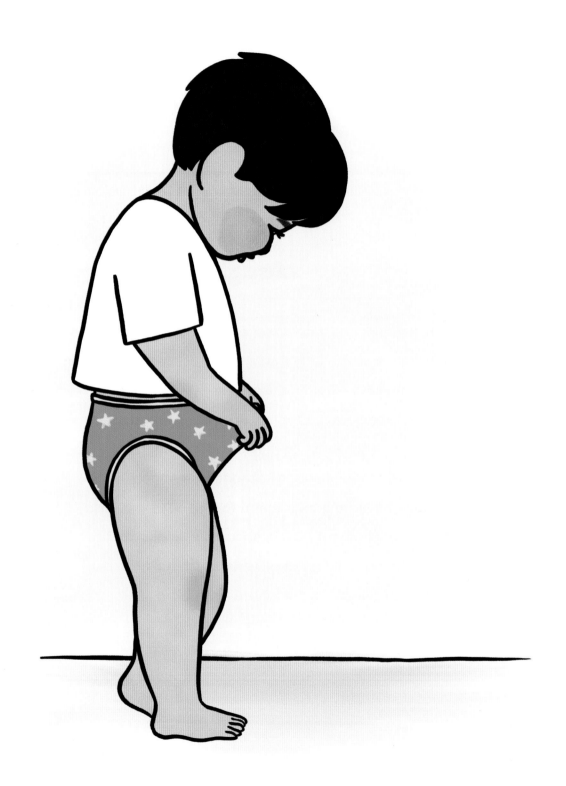

Maybe you have a penis. Maybe someone in your family has a penis. Maybe you're curious to learn more about penises. A penis is a very interesting part of the body!

Lots of people have penises! Penises can look many different ways. Some penises are longer or shorter. Some are very straight, and others curve. Penises are lots of different skin colors. However a penis looks is just right for that penis!

Some penises have layers of skin over the end called a foreskin, like these.

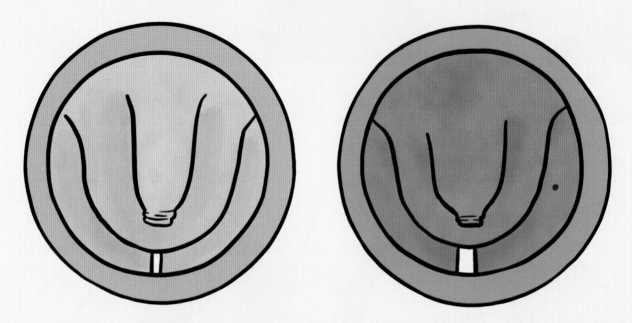

Other penises have the foreskin removed
(this is done soon after a baby is born), like these.

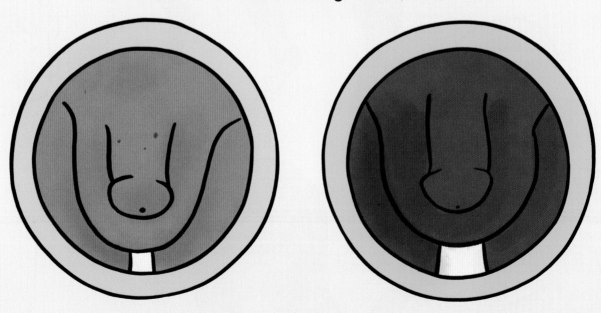

Penises have a few different parts.

   The base of the penis is where it attaches to the body. The shaft is the part in the middle.

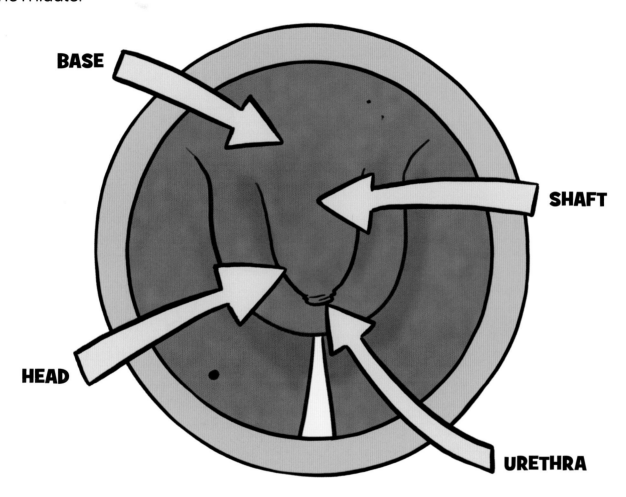

The head of the penis is the part at the end. Isn't it funny that people call it a head? It looks pretty different from your head that has your nose and ears!

   Another part is a little opening called the urethra, which is usually at the end of the head. (The entire urethra is actually a small tube inside the body, and this opening is the very end of the tube.)

Teenagers and grown-ups usually have some hair around the base of the penis. Children don't have hair there.

Under the penis is a sac called the scrotum. Inside of it are two organs shaped like little balls. They're called testes, or testicles. The scrotum and testes are usually very sensitive—they want you to be gentle with them!

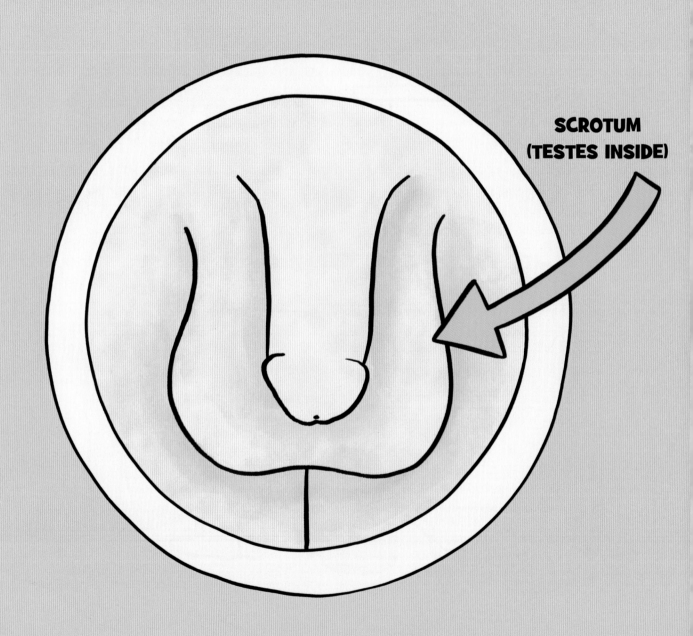

**SCROTUM
(TESTES INSIDE)**

Penises can do some pretty interesting things.

The penis is where pee comes out. Pee comes out of the end of the urethra, which looks like a little hole.

Many people stand up when they use their penis to pee. Some prefer to sit down sometimes, or all the time.

The grown-up word for pee is urine.

Another hole is behind the scrotum. It's called the anus, and it's where poop comes out.

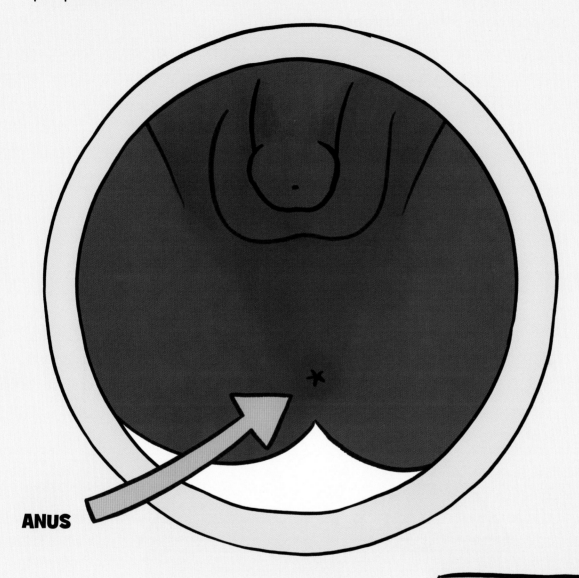

ANUS

Some people call all these parts of the body "private parts." It's okay to touch these body parts when you're in private, in a place with no other people, like in your bedroom or the bathroom at home.

Sometimes penises get a little bigger and stick out or up more for a little while. That's called an erection. It might feel good, strange, uncomfortable, or funny. However it feels, it's normal. Erections are something most penises do.

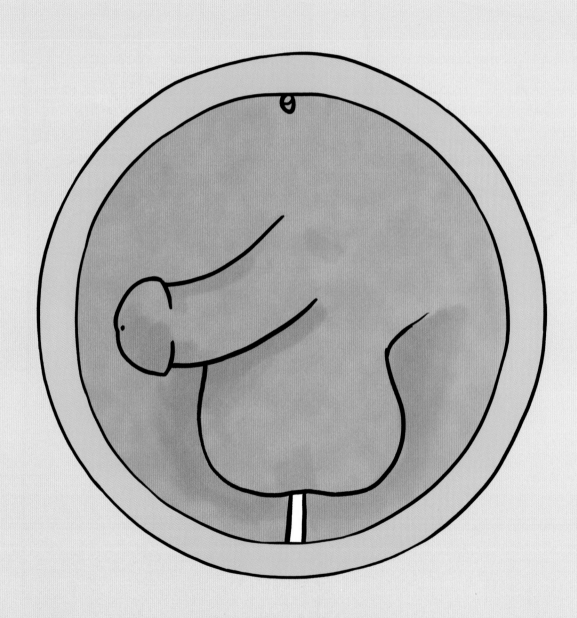

Remember the scrotum, down under the penis? Sometimes the scrotum pulls in tighter or hangs farther from the body. Usually it moves closer when it's cold—it helps the testes snuggle in to stay warm!

And it hangs down lower if it's hot to help the testes stay cooler.

Testes have a very important job for grown-ups if they want to make a baby.
That's because testes make sperm.

Sperm are teeny, tiny cells that look like this—but they are so small you need a microscope to see them. Sperm from the testes and penis can join together with a tiny egg from another person.

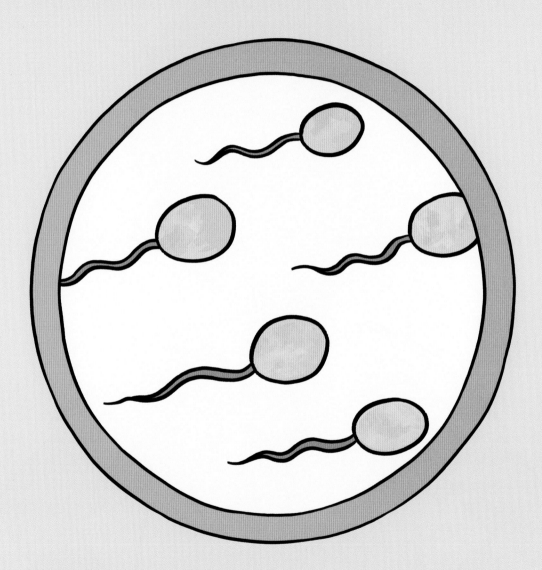

If a sperm and egg join, that's how a baby can begin to grow! Children's bodies do not make sperm.

The penis is a private part of the body. It is always okay to say no if someone wants to touch a private part of your body.

It's very important not to keep touching a secret, even if someone tells you to. If you aren't sure about someone touching you or you feel mixed-up, you may decide to talk to a grown-up you trust, like a parent, a grandparent, a teacher, or a neighbor.

Penises are just another part of the body, like elbows, chins, or toes. But penises are also pretty special. They do things that no other body part can do.

It's good to learn
all about penises!

Additional Information for Parents and Caregivers

How to be an askable parent:

Use the correct words for body parts. Give short, honest answers to your child's questions about bodies and sexuality, then ask, "Did that answer what you wanted to know?" It's okay to say, "I need to think more about how to answer that," but follow up with an answer promptly.

Most of all, remember that one hundred 1-minute conversations about sexuality topics will make more of an impact than one 100-minute conversation. Everyday life presents constant opportunities to share your values, observations, and information with your child.

Is this book only for children with penises?

Definitely not! We believe it's important for all children to learn about penises, vulvas, and vaginas in all their diversity. However, we recognize that these subjects may be of interest at different times and in different contexts, which is why we created two separate books. We hope you'll also explore *All About Vulvas and Vaginas* together, if you haven't already!

About how babies are made:

While *All About Penises* touches on the idea that testes produce sperm that can be part of starting a baby, this is certainly a subject that should be explained in more detail now or later. We believe that three-to-seven-year-old children are old enough to begin to understand how babies are made and born. While some children will ask lots of questions, others never ask, in which case it's up to the parent or caregiver to start the conversation or choose a book on the subject to read together.

It can be helpful to point out to children that all babies start from sperm, an egg, and a uterus where the embryo grows. And after they are born, all babies need a person or people to love and care for them. These elements can come together many different ways. The same two grown-ups may fill all the roles, or other people may be part of how a baby came to be, as in the case of adoption; surrogacy; sperm, egg, or embryo donation; or other assisted reproductive technologies.

Taking care of penises that have foreskins:

Usually, a baby's foreskin does not retract. At some point while growing up, though, the foreskin begins to retract, meaning it slides back and forth easily over the head of the penis. For some children, this begins during the preschool years; for others, not until they are teens. This wide range is normal. Never try to forcibly retract a foreskin—this can cause damage. For health reasons, it's important that the foreskin can be pulled back all the way by adulthood.

You can ask your child to check and tell you if the skin can slide. If it can, instruct them to slide it back when they pee so urine doesn't get trapped between the foreskin and head of the penis.

Also, once the foreskin can be retracted, it is important to pull it back and clean gently underneath it with warm water (no soap needed) when they take a bath or shower. When they finish washing, they should slide the foreskin back to its usual position. As a parent or caregiver, you can remind your child to wash under their foreskin, the same way you remind them to wash their neck or hair.

About erections:

It is common for babies and young children to experience erections. They may experience these as alarming, uncomfortable, or even painful, and need reassurance that this experience is normal and temporary. You can teach your child that if an erection feels uncomfortable under clothing, it can help if they change the penis's position so it's pointing up. Penises don't begin to ejaculate until puberty.

About masturbation:

As any preschool or early elementary school teacher can attest, it's common for young children to discover that touching their genitals feels good. Rather than shaming children that their touching is "bad" or "dirty," parents and caregivers should redirect children matter-of-factly, teaching them that this is something to be done in private (and explaining what that word means). This book does not teach the word masturbation, but parents may choose to introduce this word.

About intersex bodies:

Not all bodies are the same! Some people are born intersex. This term means a person's body may be different from what we think of as a "girl body" or a "boy body" in terms of genitals, chromosomes, internal reproductive organs, hormone levels, or DNA. This is part of the enormous diversity of ways bodies can be.

About private parts and preventing sexual abuse:

This book takes a trauma-informed approach in how it addresses consent and the possibility of sexual abuse. Sexual abuse prevention must be primarily the responsibility of adults, not children.

Advocates now understand that the old message to "say no and tell someone right away" is unrealistic for many children and potentially harmful. Because it's common that the person who sexually abuses a child is someone they love or depend on, most children who are sexually abused are never able to say no, and many later carry tremendous guilt that they were unable to end the abuse.

It's important to emphasize to children that they are in charge of their own bodies and have the right to say no, as well as ensuring they know that being touched by someone else should never be a secret. Many children who have been sexually abused report feeling confused or mixed-up, and may feel more comfortable "asking for help" rather than "telling," since they may feel concerned about getting themselves or the other person in trouble.

Talking with kids about their bodies in age-appropriate ways can be part of helping to keep them safe. A child whose vocabulary about their body shows self-awareness is less vulnerable to anyone who is looking for children to target. Knowing body-part names could help a child be able to describe accurately what happened if abuse ever did occur. Most importantly, talking openly with your child demonstrates for them that these topics can be discussed, and that you are a person whom they can trust with their questions and concerns.

Check out the other books in this series, and also our recommendations
for other children's books on related topics, at learningaboutbodies.com.